THE WOUNDED WINDS

BEN YOUNES MAJEN

Book Cover Image by Banksy

Alwan Arabiya Publications

alwanarabiya@gmail.com

© 2021 MAJEN, BEN YOUNES
Förlag: BoD – Books on Demand, Stockholm, Sverige
Tryck: BoD – Books on Demand, Norderstedt, Tyskland
ISBN: 9789178519682

BEN YOUNES MAJEN

THE WOUNDED WINDS

AN IMMIGRANT'S NOTE BOOK

POEMS

TRANSLATED FROM THE FRENCH BY:

XIAOWEI BOND

TO MY FAMILY

Acknowledgement

Many thanks to Salima and Jonathan for
revising the first draft.

I was born an orphan

Amidst other orphans

God created our parents

Society conceived a home for the
abandoned

At this home of stifling misery

Drunken with my own tears hot and
salty

I suffer in this raucous eternity

In Oujda, Lyon, Paris and London

I witnessed the light arising behind the
Moroccan horizon

But it was soon darkened

By the nocturnal solitude

Within which I saw only the oblivion

I have been living in endurance and
sufferance

Hand to my mouth, under the shadow
of a gigantic spider

Sprawling over a sunken wall

In my dreams of dawns

I await with fervor, the hollows days fall

Time passed swiftly in languor

I saw birth of evasive days

Such was my monotonous refuge

Such was the end of my opaque space

Each day I sank deeper into the
wreckage

Of the vacuous abyss

Under an insufferable pain

Engulfed in my furtive tears

I saw birth of universe and its eclipse

Its somber and abstract silence
tormented my spirit

In my dreams, I have succumbed
thousand times

Without regaining consciousness

But the sanctuary of my existence

Had become apathetic

I, who search euphoria in the stars

Of this universe far away

Like the calm of the nonchalant nights

I let go of a mordant sigh

Under the arc of disarray

I feel this desire to live, and to relive

Once again, my unhappy and sparing
childhood days

I always believed that the unfinished
human duel

Must save the archaic stimulation

And the ancient evil that the universe
exerted upon us

And the total negation of the individual

To convince this society of recluses

Here I was again,

In quest of incense in the center of my enigma,

There I found self-interest in my divine destiny,

I was thereafter insipid

Blinded by hatred,

So intense that my heart pounded at a casual love

But I did not wish to die

Without acquiring the transcendental wisdom

Because I abhor lies

Subdued by the doctrine of contempt and of sorcery

At giant's steps, the time reversed
across the migrating twilight

O, wise king of the torrential rain,

Of the streaming rivers, of gigantic
mountains, of rebellious wind of the
vagabonds

For you only

I licked my wounds and the injury of my
invisible sighs

O, wise king!

My life is an extended sunflower upon
an island

Washed by waves under a dormant sun

I am like a perfidious soul

Betrayed by the old age of the impotent
time

In front of your mystic gaze

I extinguished my reticent furor

Drowned myself in the emptiness of London

When will the torch of grace shed light?

On my mountains of doubt?

Someone said to me: calm yourself!

But how do I calm down?

Forget the pains inflicted by the
delusion?

Forget the ill-fated sufferance?

The taciturn and melancholic emotion

In front of entombed human condition

I suffered so much in those faded days,

Since long time,

I was alone to sow the seeds of confusion

Between French mutism (silence)

English eloquence

And Arabic rhetoric

Although the verses emanated from my writing

And the erratic structures were to be ruthlessly censored

In chasing the intrepid battle of the
London fog,

Which has defaced the eternal sky,

I remember the atrocity of the
hazardous seas

Where foam of my life was washed
away by the angry waves

Incarcerated between two virgin stars

The forbidden fruit to foreigners

Sank deep into this muddy world

Rain or snow covering my immense sky

I came to offer you my odyssey

I came to sing you my rhapsody

As an innocent prey,

I was blinded by a condemned love.

Who are you, day of enslaved solitude?

Who sent you to me?

You, the deaf mute, have you reached
the age of reasoning

For understanding the rhythm of the
silence?

Whereas to me, I am accustomed to the
shackled thirst,

Where lugubrious autumn of quivering
and withered leaves

Rendered me vague satisfaction

Here I am, an immigrant against my will,

Dissipated in this impregnable citadel,

My anguished itinerary

Like a stray cat under a twinkling star

Dancing to the rhythm of the dawn of a
No-Man's Land

Immortal glory to the living thinkers of a
locked Utopia,

Who are dying under the gag of the
bestial justice?

And under the deceiving eyes of a
gliding vulture

Glory to the sanguine spirits,

Glory to the mordant lips without
rancor,

Glory to the feelings buried in this
eternal infinity.

Immigrants of all nations, unleash your
reins,

But do not turn back the bridles.

All these years, I shared with you the fruit

Of my sorrow and my humble offering.

O Sidi-Yahya, Sage of all sages,

Lend me a beautiful Houria, and a magic flute,

Wild with passion,

For tomorrow, I shall leave for the unknown

Where no one awaits me,

To the land where all bitter seasons vanish.

I bless the sea of flame

This sea of carnage massacred

And decapitated by the raging waves

With their woeful chanting rites,

Revived my memory of that intoxicating time

Echo by echo.

Orphaned since the age of three severe winters,

I was born to taste the humble pie

Of the monotonous sufferance.

One taught me to dream,

But nights were too ephemeral

Where foretelling stars clash with each other.

My moist voice, chocking from time to time,

Grazes the empty fringe (of my throat)

Which irritates me to let go my sotto voce (suppressed) curses.

I am baptised by the foams of Mediterranean snow

And the shadows of virgin seasons.

I was taught to write the words and
rhythm,

I was taught that the human pride is a
voice

Tamed by the desire of succulent and
poisonous feat

My voice with ruptured flow of fluid

Which became agitated in the night

As a gush of blood

As a relentlessly burning furnace

In the bright fires of destiny and of
passion.

I was born in a labyrinth where tears and sweat clash into each other

In a criss-crossing deluge

I was told that my voice was like a source

Inundated by the thirsty Apocalypse

I was born, for certain, to liberate my voice,

My longings, and my emotion.

The elders of the village N'gadi

Gave me enlightening advice

To rid of the boredom and the lingering nightmare.

I left my village without their blessings

I left them my sac of bric-a-brac full of
holes

My only companion was a talisman with
the engravings

Of the beggars of Souk-al-Joutiya

I became disoriented like a lame lark

I pursued all roads to hell and to Avatar

A foreboding invaded me, crushing my heart

So long, the oppressive loneliness and hopelessness

Good morning, the folly of dizzy dreams

In my intoxication,

I met happiness in tatters

Sun of Vengeance,

I curse you of your scorching rays

Sun of God,

You heightened my painful endurance

A faint glimmer of a balmy morning
witnessed my flight.

My exile was predicted by stars and
spectres.

I played truant at school,

They forced me to read repeatedly the
intoned rites.

With my bleeding quill,

I killed my shadow on the scornful pages
of my diaries.

Under the pillars of the village N'gadi

And the jagged shadows of virgin palms
of Oujda.

During those years, I ran and ran

In search of wandering Mistral wind.

You, the elders of the village, images of
congealed blood,

You tarnished my mirror with seven
scratches,

Seven years of misfortune.

You, the sages, the breeders of Black
Widows

Of the thousand decapitated beggars.

I am the angel of the nothingness with
misty eyes,

You are the chimera of treason and of
deception.

I am the migrating bird chased by the castrated vultures.

I was on the roads of Oujda,

That were scorched by its crushing sun

Swept by its violent Sirocco.

City of ramparts ravaged by impetuous hurricane

City of the legend masked by sand and blood.

You evoked me of the dreams of disarray.

You rebuffed my fatherly love.

I become your forgotten past

Your silence and your perpetual insomnia.

I met all the new 'Mohas' of this foreign
world

I took all the lucrative risks.

I discovered that all the mules of my
village

Have been condemned to the daily
slavery,

And all the people of Oujda suffered
persistent pain.

At our house, 'he who changes his place
loses his skin'

Only the hardship hides his game.

I hear of speaking of the errant abyss

Where the distant sea undulates

I hear of speaking of dark waves

Who drove the cursed swamp to
melancholy?

I hear speaking of Freudian dreams

Mutilated by the besieged gladiators.

I hear speaking of the 'Private Zone'

Where the 'No-man's Land' unfolding in
wandering.

I hear speaking of the juveniles who
blatantly

Impersonate a flagrant delinquency

Incarcerated under the insidious locks of
the isolated walls

I hear speaking of the tumultuous and
starless nights

Where the endurance sway in front of
my tired eyes.

In front of me, the barbed-wired roads

Dissipated under my nonchalant steps

I hear speaking of "Beurs"

And their unhealthy huts in shantytown

At Nanterre or elsewhere

Who live in the margin of the society?

In the cardboard box city

With mouldy cartoon 'Made in France'

I hear speaking of their troubled
existence

Where the Melanesians, the castaways
and the undesirables

Of Maghreb are being locked in
between walls

Never being able to reach the human
Zenith.

Today, I have become a scarred Epicurean

By the incursion of the painful solitude.

My burning skin tattooed under the whips of the executioner

And the torturers who harassed me day after day.

Angry at the enchanted Utopia

I, the insurgent angel at the crucified silhouette

Under the nursed pain

I, the vengeful angel of black fury

Which cries day and night:

Atrocity, atrocity, and atrocity!

Our children were burned

Mercilessly and pitilessly,

But the pure soul never burns

That for saving our shackled eternity!

On my epitaph, someone wrote:

Here lies: Liberty, Fraternity, and
Equality!

Silence is a haunted tomb

Silence is an unnatural muteness.

In this simple life

I have crossed over the oblivion and
solitary illusion.

My soul is an open window of an
uncharted land

Horizon is a space of infinity.

At home the profound pain

Is a locked canvas.

The soul of a locked poet.

The soul of a poet is a landscape

Abstract and unfinished on a canvas.

My youth was like a sleep

Of unforgettable nightmare.

A choral singing of the ephemeral
twilight.

The silence is a pitiless sufferance.

The silence is a prison

On an island without horizon

Who are you, my vivacious love?

Only a song of a troubadour and a
vagabond!

An unfinished poem

And without inspiration.

A broken lute

And without vibrations

Abandoned by the 'Maddah'

Of a thousand and one nights.

Who are you, the sunken love?

Only a flag in half-mast

In my effervescent heart!

Why do you torment me?

Why do you lure me?

Why so much rancour?

I have escaped your dominant lassitude.

Precocious love, enchained love

I ask myself who are you?

Do you remember the river of desire?

Where the enchanting dawn

Bathed upon us

Our love unleashes like a cascade of joy
and a passion

And the innocent grass witnessed our
tender heartbeat.

I spent all my life tormenting the cynical
mirrors.

Our existence is controlled

By a slow pendulum in the emptiness.

Your body on my bed

Like a canvas falling of sky,

Bewitched by a celestial angel.

Paris embraces London

London extinguishes in light and fog

Which transform in a rainbow.

To survive the evil of identity

I have to burn my mask

Tear apart your uproarious silence

Caress your sad injury

And count your reeling wounds

Collect your ashes

And go away, far away…far away

Until you reach the twilight of your enclosed soul.

They have set fire to an inferno

Take your wind and your logs and
disappear

Take your rain and inundate the enlaced
isles.

Take your centuries and ride towards
eternity

Where fear and silence dissipate.

Go and join the recluses of the 'No-
Man's Land'

Who strayed in the nothingness and the
enigma!

I am no longer the master of the
Sepulchre inferno

I no longer belong to the invisible
miracles,

I am the galloping mirage.

I am the smothered light at sombre
eyes.

Like the nights of the temerarious
sufferance,

I am a heartless fare-well

Without solace angels

Who resuscitate the perturbed death?

And the eclipse of the treacherous
waves.

With my felt pen

I enter the obscurity,

My body martyred by the defeated
submission.

Alone, I pile up the burned frontier

With my pen of blood and ink

I grafted my destiny on the corpse of
stagnant time.

My dawn was ardent

My deluge was not like others

Under sly stars

I burned my clay pen

I became a wounded dream

Without cloud

Without horizon,

Without refuge

I am the lord of sterile speech

I am the shadow

Who doesn't palpitate at the distant
sun?

To which the field vanished

With my frustrated silence

I crossed the dunes of vagabonds

I deserted the hollow roads

And I abandoned my wounds

Trembling in the songs of loneliness.

Shadow of vengeful devil across the mutilated horizon

Reminded me of the death of an anguished soul.

From then, the baptism of fire never took place,

So that the scornful silence remains fierce.

I plunged in a sombre dream at the bottom of my pain

This mighty burden which bent my back,

And intoxicated the furnace of passion

Of hatred and of abandon.

The lightening of insurgence blasted on

The exile at Goutte d'Or, at Harlem and Brixton

Will it stir up again?

This furnace of diving offering

This thundering anger by a feverish rage

This unfinished hellish duel

I, an insignificant immigrant with ardent
heart

At heartrending cries

I came to offer you all my fatal wounds

I penetrated the obscurity of my
perturbed destiny.

I overturned the clouds and fog over
many skies

I survived the malaise against the odious
human resistance

I brought my camouflaged face

By a haunting memory of the past

But you stifled my culture,

My praise, my serene prayers

You effaced my existence and my
traditional value

You crushed my dignity and my honour

Ungratefully and pitilessly,

You ignored my presence

You spread your xenophobia with
repugnance

But I came to your home to search for
your golden promise,

I am deceived by your imaginary
allusion.

Believe me, I am not here to throw away
my defiance,

But simply to avoid the mourning of
millennium time,

I know however, that your breath a
different air.

Writer of class and of excellence

I congratulate you

For your audacity and your humanity.

Bohemian writer of torture and of wisdom,

You are either Cinderella or a sword.

Horizon is in flame,

Hatred and excitement

Imperishable glory

You are sometimes unknown to the displaced face

Writer of crazy passion

You are a hero crucified on the unspeakable ecstasy

You bring a suffocated lute

You exist in human drunkenness.

When you die on a thread of evasion

Idolatry rivalling against each other.

You are an untouchable heavenly body

But you cease to be the weakness of
timorous pages

And the arrogance of shackled tyrants,

Nothing adheres to your invulnerable
glory.

I greet your ubiquity

Writer of lustrous times

You open all the veiled doors,

You intoxicate all the reflections of
mirrors

Where scintillate ideas scatter.

You are like a sultan

Obsessed with a thousand and one
nights,

You are the ultimate cavalier

I congratulate you heartily

Immigrant you are only a scapegoat

A drowned drop in a solitary ocean

An unknown non-entity

In a city pregnant of hate and of despise

Immigrant, your presence has become
undesirable,

Under the shallow sky

You are enslaved in your sanctuary,

Faced with ungrateful and miserable
persons

Who never keep their promise?

And who quickly forget their vows of
prowess

At their home, you are just a lukewarm
sun

On a savage swamp of boredom

Muddied by the aborted toad

You are just a defeated spectacle

A dream of bound solitude

Immigrant, it suffices to shake the fan of wounded winds

To plunder their toothless trees.

City of misty silhouettes

City of reticent souls,

I came to shake off my nightmare

I came to graze my languid desire,

My ride on oriental horseback

And my eternal emptiness.

I can see only a reflection of my fleeting memories

Reattached to your distant mirage.

Am I a solitary dawn?

Or am I an exiled meteor?

A migrant shadow from nowhere?

City of wounded feeling, the tomb of crumpled flowers,

And of stray dunes,

When the fringe of your tenuous wave

Crushes the tentacles of tempestuous
storm,

When my sighs and my wounds

Hamper your naked abyss

It's time to exit from the ashes of the
Phoenix.

In my funeral corner,

I smothered my little mirage,

My light is dim,

My spark is frail,

My silence stiffened

And my vision wandered on the
riverbank

Like a dream of effervescent chimera,

Alone, on the doorstep of my enclosure.

I originate from this swamp of space

Drowsy in a foul circle,

The thunder and the blast of hurricane,

Surround the remains of my dark village

Your sarcophagus of requiem saddened
me.

We must penetrate our musty exile,

We must extol ourselves of the
incandescence,

Our seedling engendered a sheathed
passion,

Aroused our aspiration.

The colour of our thickened blood

Annihilated us.

It's the nothingness that stimulate our
place in this world

And the nostalgia of our quarters of clay
haunts us forever.

Ben Younes Majen

Ben Younes Majen was born in 1946 in Oujda, Morocco. He is a retired civil servant and currently living in London. In 1968 he left Morocco for France as a contracted manual worker, but in 1970 he moved from Paris to London.

Ben Younes Majen writes poetry in Arabic, French, and English. As a matter of fact, he started writing poetry at the age of eighteen and has published nineteen books of poetry, sixteen of them in Arabic, two in French, and one in English.

Ben's experience of both cultural differences and different cultures has influenced much of his poetry.
Most of his poems are written in free verse and structured around his life as

an immigrant.

His poems range over a variety of subjects, settings, scenes, and cultural awareness, such as misery, suffering, and pain of others in the Arab World.

Ben Younes Majen is based in London and holds an MA in translation studies from the University of Westminster.

Förlag: BoD – Books on Demand, Stockholm, Sverige
Tryck: BoD – Books on Demand, Norderstedt, Tyskland
ISBN: 9789178519682